RISING FROM THE ASHES

LEA MORENO SANTANA

© 2017 by Lea Moreno Santana

Rising From the Ashes

ISBN-13: 978-0-692-69834-1

Published in San Antonio, Texas by Lea Moreno Santana.

Edited by The Innovative Pen, Mari Moreno, Stephanie Mion, and Deidre Sequeira

Cover art by Jakob Santana

Scripture quotations marked NLT are from the *Holy Bible*, New Living Translation, copyright © 1996, 2004. Used by permission of Tyndale House Publisher, Inc., Carol Stream, Illinois 60188. All rights reserved.

ISBN-13: 978-1-4143-0709-1

Scripture quotations marked NIV are taken from the Holy Bible, *New International Version®, NIV®*. Copyright © 1973, 1978, 1984 by Biblica, Inc.™ Used by permission of Zondervan. All rights reserved worldwide.

ISBN-13: 978-0-310-94900-8

Quotations from "The Five Love Languages" by Gary Chapman are used with permission of Northfield Publishing. Copyright © 1992, 1995, 2004.

ISBN-13: 98-1-881273-15-8

I gladly dedicate this book to my husband, Ariel Santana, my two sons, Jakob and Lukas, and my beautiful angel in heaven. Thank you all for being such a great support system.

CONTENTS

ACKNOWLEDGMENTS

I would like to express my special thanks to a few individuals who took part in the completion of this book and helping me get where I am today. I would like to thank Antoinette Dickson, Mari Moreno, Stephanie Mion, Deidre Sequeira, and Daqri Bernardo for taking time to read, proofread, and assist in the editing of *Rising from the Ashes*. I would like to thank Jakob Santana for creating a cover that accurately represents what I tried to convey in the book about my life. Thank you for understanding what was difficult to express. I would like to thank my parents, Gilbert and Mari Moreno, for supporting me along the way. Thank you for always keeping me in your prayers and demonstrating that we are overcomers and victorious in our pursuits. To my church family at Restoring Hope Church of God, thank you for your prayers and support. Lastly, I want to thank my family Ariel, Jakob, and Lukas Santana for being part of this journey. I will always appreciate how you all continued to encourage me despite the times my stresses took me away from family fun time, home cooked meals, and just time away from you in general.

It has been a long and difficult journey, but it was all worth it. As you can see, it has taken me years to finally say it's time for me to complete this project, but God knew when it was time to move forward. Although many say we are a "reality show" family, they have no idea how much better we are than that. I only hope the story of mine and my family's perseverance can show others that, when things may look as if they are in disarray, there is always true HOPE!

RISING FROM THE ASHES

PROLOGUE

"To all who mourn in Israel, he will give a crown of beauty for ashes, a joyous blessing instead of mourning, festive praise instead of despair. In their righteousness, they will be like great oaks that the LORD has planted for his own glory."
    Isaiah 61:3 (NLT)

Many may think that they have a messy life, but I have come to terms with my mess being a message. I remember a time in my life when I would be so upset because I woke up. Today, it saddens my heart to imagine not being able to watch my children grow up; how, in the midst of my storm, I would have brought everyone down with me. God is so good and He wanted me to overcome this because I needed to help others. In my mind, I could never see this day. All I could see was the darkness in my life. I remember always saying, "I'm living in hell. I just want to die." God had so many plans for me. I am now able to speak to others about my situation and how they don't have to give up. Don't get me wrong, I will go through many things (as we all do) and my past may come knocking at my door, but I now know God is with me.

My last attempt to take my life was when my younger son was eight. As my story progresses, I will share more about my life during that time. I had begun to feel as if I was alone, with no desire to push myself towards doing anything. My parents have always been the type of parents who support their children, but because of where I was mentally and spiritually, I wouldn't let them into my world, thus isolating myself and making things worse. In retrospect, I also believe it was because I was afraid of disappointing them.

My focus wasn't to better myself. My goal was to live in the familiar discomfort of my misery. At that time, I couldn't explain its source. I longed to understand, but that understanding would not come for many years.

LET IT RAIN

CHAPTER I

"Watch your tongue and keep your mouth shut, and you will stay out of trouble."

Proverbs 21:23 (NLT)

Some of my greatest childhood memories are of my parents. One of those familiar memories was walking into my mother's room as she was on her knees praying. My parents have always been strong in their faith. They taught us to always go to God in prayer. Not only were they spiritually strong and leaders in the church, they were also very loving and always supportive of their children. Despite all this love and support, I couldn't find myself. As much as I longed to share the same sense of belonging that my siblings had, it never happened. I never had a close friend because I feared I was not good enough. I knew about God, but I didn't *know* God, and I certainly didn't know what He could do for me. I just could not connect with God like everyone else and didn't know what He could do in and through me. I didn't understand that having a connection with God would bring me to life and would give me the strength that I needed.

Fourth grade can be quite enjoyable for a child. As I question my son, Luke, about his fourth grade experiences, he mentions everything with a sense of excitement. He talks about having many friends, and never mentions fears, not having fun, or any problems. His experiences were definitely different from my own.

Two events as a fourth grader changed my life tremendously. As I mentioned before, my parents were very involved with our local church region. Often, they would have to attend different events out of town. On one such occasion, I was really looking forward to staying with my favorite uncle. I was excited because my cousins would be there. Our family always played board games, and I was so excited to play. That excitement ended when I was stuck trying to find a word.

The funny thing was that I had my little sister with me, and for some reason, that always made me feel safe. I knew I would be okay. We began playing Scrabble and soon, I was having some issues. Being unable to figure out a word to put down in Scrabble may be common for most, but this was more than that for me.

∾

"Are you stupid or what?"

Growing up, I always had a hard time in my studies. Mom and Dad would sit with us while we did our homework. I remember my father giving us pop quizzes, which he tried to make a fun event for us. I never had fun, because I would always get the answer wrong. As I remember it, the game was as follow: we would stand up with our hands up and if we got the answer correct, one arm would go down and so forth. I would see my siblings going on to the next level and my arms were still up. Pop didn't do it so that we would feel bad, it was supposed to be fun for everyone. You know how you feel when you're always the last one to get picked? That exact feeling came over me, often. Mom would check our homework and circle the incorrect answers, and we knew we had to make corrections. I would cry because she had to explain the answers to me. The more she attempted to explain, the more the tears would fall, and eventually, I would try to hide. We spent many late hours at the table, just the two of us, with her doing her best to help me understand, and me doing my best to get her to realize that I wasn't comprehending it.

Going back to scrabble, I had been stuck trying to come up with a word for what seemed like eternity. My uncle finally yelled, "Whose turn is it?" My sister answers, "Lea's." The next five words to leave his mouth left me crushed and in tears. "Are you stupid or what?" I cried softly, as if they couldn't see me. My parents would never insult me in that manner, so why did he insult me with those ugly words? My favorite uncle crushed me so bad that, since that day, I held on to his terrible words and accepted them.

I remember going to bed that night, still crying. My sister thought I was crying because I missed mom and dad. I wasn't blue; I was miserable, and I felt stupid. That evening greatly affected my relationship with my uncle and served to deepen my insecurities. My favorite uncle had crushed my spirit, and, from that moment on, I accepted that I must be "stupid or something." I held onto that belief.

I didn't understand why anyone would say that to a child. My mom would never have lost her patience with any of us, never uttered those words to me, even after having to explain the same thing nearly one hundred times. Whatever his reasoning, I carried the pain of his words into adulthood. Finally, years ago, I was truly able to forgive him. Although he had passed, I allowed myself to let go of the hurt, but this was only possible with God's help.

Another occasion that my life was changed tremendously was in the classroom. My fourth grade teacher was constantly yelling. Now, I come from a family that speaks loud. Oh, did I forget to mention I speak very loudly, as well? As my insecurities began to manifest themselves, I began to find myself easily startled by things, even if they had nothing to do with me.

Although I could speak quite loudly, I was becoming a very quiet introvert who was eager to please. I did everything the teacher asked. Coming in from recess one day, the teacher was shouting at us, again. She began telling us how upset she was and that we were a terrible class. I took that to heart, as if she was telling me that personally. I began to cry, and the little kids at my table giggled and told the teacher. She came to my table and stated that she wasn't yelling at me. She then ordered me to the restroom to wipe my face. That only made things worse. Now, I had to deal with the embarrassment of my classmates calling me a baby. I pretended to be sick for the entire week, crying daily to go to the nurse.

Memories from the past have a way of holding us captive. Instead of facing them and moving forward, we allow fear to prevent our progress. A major part of my issue was that I didn't know how to let go. Things seemed to happen repeatedly. Letting go just didn't seem to be a viable option. This affected many of my relationships. Instead of dealing with the problem at hand, I swept it under the rug. In the years that have passed, God alone has been the one that could comfort me in ways no friend, parent, sibling, or man ever could. He continues to fill voids daily and assures me when I doubt.

As a child, I couldn't understand why adults would hurt someone so young, without realizing or caring that they were doing so. As an adult, I can say how these things affected me, but I can also see how the words we say to someone can affect them as an adult. Our words are so powerful they can kill one's soul. I am careful with my words now, but I still struggle at times, and that memory always comes back as a tool.

I'm hopeful that my nephews and nieces will one day understand why I am quick to speak out against people making fun of others. I know in life that we must learn to roll with the punches, but I don't believe in doing so at the stake of negatively influencing someone's future. I want them to understand the power of their words. Some may wonder why I didn't stand up for myself. To be quite honest, I couldn't understand why it seemed that no one came to my defense. However, my hurt and confusion had me consumed and distracted; therefore, it is most likely that I wouldn't have noticed if someone did come to my defense. Many years would pass before I learned the truth: God is my defender. Wow... God is MY defender. As hard as it may be for you to grasp that concept, I am telling you from experience that it is an absolute truth.

BULLY

CHAPTER II

"Bad company corrupts good character."
1 Corinthians 15:33 (NIV)

My introduction to seventh grade was "I will do it." I uttered those words when a "friend" asked me to beat up another classmate. This was the beginning of me being a bully. There was a young girl that was hated by everyone for some unknown reason. Everyone wanted her out of our groups and honestly, even to this day, I don't know why. I come from a family of boxers (my pop's side of the family). I was very proud, so why not knock someone out if my uncles always did? My uncles didn't box for the same reason I was choosing to box; I chose to use my hands as weapons. Wow, another Moreno in the ring and I'm a girl. I remember going to the ring and my brothers sparing. I was still a quiet girl, but I wanted to feel accepted in every part of my life. I was getting attention at home, as always, but didn't feel as if I was.

Every time my friends wanted me to do something, I said I would do it, regardless of how bad it was. I didn't realize what repercussions and hurt would come out of listening to a person that I thought was brave, someone who had asked someone else to fight for her. How brave is that? What I just couldn't understand is that by trying to belong, the only ones that accepted me were the bully type of friends. The bully leader knows how vulnerable other kids are, and they take little bites of them until nothing is left.

I wanted to be accepted in every part of my life. My family is a musical family; the majority of them play an instrument, write music, teach music or sing. I started to play the clarinet in band, because everyone else was playing in the band at home. I would see my parents go to all the band concerts, football games, or wrestling matches. I wanted to belong. I didn't know what I liked or if it was alright to like anything. No matter how much my parents showed love and support, I still struggled with acceptance and that carried over into my life at school.

~

It wasn't me

There were several times in middle school that I would find myself fighting with other classmates on the field or behind a building. Every time my friends wanted me to do something that they didn't want to do (regardless of how bad it was), I would do it. Gaining their approval made my ears sharper to their wants. I was always saying it wasn't my fault and that they made me do it. In church, I began to separate our groups as well, because I wanted everyone to be my friend. Don't get me wrong, the most fun I had was at church. Granted, I was more concerned about having fun than anything related to God. I loved to get together with the youth and go skating, bowling, to amusement parks and camp outings. Nothing that I was doing made me feel remorseful or think that "I'm being mean" or "God wouldn't like this."

As time would go by, I was already in the eighth grade and people began to turn against me because I was a bully. They began to make fun of me because of my skin color and because I was just a bully. No one wanted to hang out with me, and every other word that came out of my mouth was foul and unacceptable. Others began to stay away from me, because they didn't like who I had become. I had so much fear of not being accepted by anyone, not just one individual, but everyone. I would react in ways that would hurt people, and I was intentional about it. I would call myself the black sheep of the family, and say that I didn't belong. The last day of school, a good friend from elementary, who had moved away, came to visit. I was too busy to pay attention to her because I was fighting with another girl. My heart sank when I found out that she was gone. Good news is that she found me recently through Facebook. I have since asked for forgiveness about how I acted with her. She doesn't recall the incident, but I do, and I believe that if she remembered it, we probably wouldn't be friends.

As I became older, I began to realize that she had a special place in my heart, and that she was one that I could call my friend. Why I ignored her may have been because I felt angry that she left me. All the insecurities from childhood spilled over to middle school leaving me with a need to be accepted. I was full of fear, insecurities, and rejection. I was looking for the attention I desired in the wrong places. I was lost, confused, and not aware of how holding onto what wasn't good would affect me. I felt I could never do anything because I was stupid. I believed what others said about me, which affected my decisions. As much as I wanted to believe that others cared for and loved me, I didn't know how to express or feel love.

While growing up, there were times that I felt unloved and at fault for things. I was making decisions based on my emotions, which caused me to react in ways that I didn't realize. I was hiding the truth of who I was from everything and everyone. The more hectic my emotions became, the more my life began to spiral out of control. Eventually, I began to act out.

LOST AND ALONE

⚜

CHAPTER III

"Don't be afraid, for I am with you. Don't be discouraged, for I am your God. I will strengthen you and help you. I will hold you up with my victorious right hand."
     Isaiah 41:10 (NLT)

She won't be with us that long! Dad sat us at the table and, through his tears, told us mom only had six months to live. What was I to do? Who was going to comb my hair? And what about homework? Who was going to sit for hours at the table and tell me, "It's okay. Let's try again." All these emotions came to me and I didn't know what to do. I wanted to run away. I just wanted to die. How could someone tell me I would never see my mom again? Life went on, and I continued going through the motions, not knowing when my mom would leave me.

Watching my mom's illness progress forced us to grow up quickly. I'm sure it took a toll on dad, as well. He made sure mom was comfortable, and had everything she desired. How he was holding up, I had no idea. We all had our share of chores to do to help around the house. Dad came home from work and prepared dinner. The children washed and ironed the clothes, in addition to preparing meals.

There were days when I would stare at my mom while she was lying in bed. It was as if her eyes were heavy with the sight of death. One day, my brother and I were in the car with my mom and we just stared at each other as her hair fell out. He would tell me to "take her in the house" as he cleaned up her hair so she wouldn't see. Mom was a godly woman and had no fear. She loved God so much, even in her pain. Mom would always write letters to us. I loved her so much and desperately wanted to tell her, but I didn't know how. I thought that if I did so, it would come across as corny.

I never remember my parents hugging me or saying "I love you." I'm sure they did, but I truly can't remember because I was so closed up. I wouldn't allow anyone in. I had issues showing affection, and could much less speak of it. I was scared to leave for school because I didn't know if she would be gone when I got home. Some days we would come home, and she would be on the floor because of a stroke or fainting. Dad taught us how to bring her back by getting some ammonia and placing it under her nose. I would see her curled up hard as a rock. We became familiar with the signs that told us she had suffered a stroke. We knew how to massage her because we had seen dad do it many times.

As a preteen, it's scary to think mom or dad will not be around. I thought my dad was superman, but I didn't really know what he was feeling. I was scared to sleep at night because I wasn't sure if mom would wake up. I would run to the room at night and put my hand under mom's nose to make sure she was breathing. That was something I had seen on TV once. I'm sure my brothers and sisters have memories of what they experienced, but I began to hate my mom.

I couldn't believe she was going to leave me, and I couldn't believe God would do this to her, or to me. God was taking her from me. I was a preteen and needed my mom. I wanted to feel loved; instead, I felt lost. I went to school just to hang out. I wasn't paying attention in class, or doing homework. I was also returning to my bullying again. I wasn't involved with anything positive or productive. Why should I bother? I felt that no one cared, and I was angry with God. I felt alone, scared, and stupid, with no love inside of me. I was going through the motions of life. Mom always gave thanks to God, and I didn't understand how she could do that. She said she was ready to die, and I hated those words. I was not ready for her to leave me, and I was not willing to pray to the God who was taking her away from me.

On the surface, I seemed to be very involved in church, but I wasn't spiritually connected. In hindsight, I understood that God had a purpose for this season of my journey. I didn't know or understand that, during this time, I was to rely on Him and only Him. These were the dating years, and the graduating years in which mom would not be a part of. My heart began to harden, and I shut myself off from God, not understanding why I was being taken through this torturous journey. God needed to work on me, but I wouldn't let him in.

Wanting love, but not feeling it, I looked for it at school. My parents didn't allow me to date, but I still managed to have my heart broken a few times. I didn't understand how people could hurt you and just go on with life. I didn't feel I could go to my mom during this time because she was going to be gone soon, leaving me like everyone else had in the past. I was scared to share my heart, because every time I had done so before it had been stripped bare.

Throughout this time, we went on with our everyday life. We had to continue to live a so-called normal life. We would go to our events that my siblings and I had. We even went on vacations, to church events, and tried to live a normal life as much as possible. Being in church was something I did because mom and dad did. It didn't mean I had a choice, because mom and dad wouldn't have it. Mom was still a great trooper through it all, but the fear was always there that she wouldn't be around.

It was becoming a recurring theme in my life. What is love? Brokenhearted and convinced that things would never get better, the shadow of darkness began to overtake me again. This led to my first suicide attempt.

My junior year of high school, my dad allowed me to date for the first time. Of course, this privilege came with rules. My dates could come to the house, church, and, with permission, we could go out. I began to date a boy from church that I had briefly known. I didn't know what love was, but thought I was in love. My mom knew (as most mother's instinct and wisdom knows) what type of boy he was, and she wanted to protect me. My parents allowed me to date him, because he was from the church. He came off as a self-centered, know it all, and that was frightening to me. I had some issues of not speaking up when I should have. I allowed people to make decisions for me in many areas of my life. This was me being a people pleaser. I was afraid that if I said what I wanted others wouldn't like it, or I would be overlooked.

I tried to speak many times but always took everyone else's lead in life choices. I lived every day in fear, feeling insecure and stupid. This boy intimidated me with his actions. I rarely spoke because I was afraid that whatever I said would come out sounding dumb. He told me things that added to my feelings of being stupid and ugly. As months went by, I remember the day he told me that he had been dating someone else while he was dating me. I was hurt so deeply that I couldn't function for the rest of the day. I didn't want to go anywhere, do anything, or be around anyone.

I did continue to date him for two years. You might ask why, but I don't have an answer. I wouldn't speak about my true feelings, because for some reason I thought I had no right to do so. I never knew when to speak. I know now that I had no business dating anyone. I had seen my parents interact and therefore, knew this was not the way a relationship was supposed to be. I went on with this roller coaster feeling for about two years before he finally got tired of it all. I was young and inexperienced, and he possibly thought I would never grow up. In my mind, I didn't have anyone to share my hurt with, unlike my siblings who had friends. I wasn't close to anyone, and no one seemed to want to be close to me. I still remember the strong feelings I had about life, more specifically, about ending my life. I found myself thinking of ways that I could cease to exist.

∾

I was angry because I woke up.

My older sister had a heart murmur, and I remember she had to take pills for her heart. I knew my mom kept all of the family's medications in her medicine cabinet. When I got home, no one else was there. I headed straight for the medicine cabinet, opened it, and seeing all the bottles of prescriptions, I grabbed every one. After taking every pill, I walked from room to room. Although I was home alone, I felt the need to say goodbye to everyone. I went to my room to lie down. I closed my eyes and went to sleep. I remember hearing noises from a distance. I heard my sister and mom come into the house. The strangest thing happened next.

I woke up.

I was fully awake, and on top of that, I was angry because I woke up. I sat up as my sister walked into the room. I ran past her to the restroom and forced myself to vomit. Not knowing what was going on, my sister came into the bathroom to help hold my hair back and comfort me. She had no idea about the overdose of pills I had taken. Everyone thought I had a stomach bug, but I knew the truth. On the inside, I was dying. I didn't want to live, and kept contemplating what else I could do to leave this world behind. What a sorry attempt at suicide. I couldn't even do that right.

I began feeling sick as months went by, but the doctors couldn't diagnosis the problem. My mom was concerned, especially given what she had endured for so long. The pain at times was unbearable to the point that I couldn't walk. The doctors tried several medications attempting to find one that would alleviate the pain and symptoms. While they were searching for a diagnosis with a positive prognosis, I didn't want them to find anything. I simply wanted to die. I had learned to be sick, and I felt I had to feel pain. I had to feel pain because who would want to love me. The opposite of love to me was pain. I spent the remainder of my junior year sick, sad, and depressed, with no desire to live.

A positive turn in my life came with getting a part time job during my senior year of high school. I was away from home more, and learning to become independent. I had blamed my parents for my breakup, because I hadn't been able to really *date*, in my opinion. I was a little girl dating someone older who got tired of dealing with me and always having to answer to my parents. With my own job, I would have my own money, and, once out of high school, I could go to college and live on my own. To be honest, I wasn't really thinking about all of that. You see, I just wanted out. I wanted to check out of life.

My mom was sick, I was sick, but I was also very lost. My life was on autopilot. I still attended and remained involved in church, and I still didn't have an intimate relationship with God. Everyone assumed I was happy with life and dealing with my illness, school, and mom quite well. I learned to be an actress in my daily life, and I was becoming good at doing so, although my heart was broken and nothing (and no one) could mend it.

WONDER YEARS

❧

CHAPTER IV

"'For I know the plans I have for you,' says the LORD. 'They are plans for good and not for disaster, to give you a future and a hope. In those days when you pray, I will listen. If you look for me wholeheartedly, you will find me. I will be found by you,' says the LORD. 'I will end your captivity and restore your fortunes. I will gather you out of the nations where I sent you and will bring you home again to you own land.'"
Jeremiah 29:11-14 (NLT)

I joined the district choir; singing was a way to escape my darkness. Oh, how I loved to sing. When I sang, it was as if everything had gone away - no pain, no depression, and no rejection. I would enter a space where no one else could enter. My sister and I decided to enter our high school talent show. This is when I decided to feel no rejection; my friends liked the way I sang. I was singing at church because I enjoyed it, not out of a spirit of worship.

In June of 1990, the choir I joined was practicing at a local church here in San Antonio, and I loved going to practice. During one of our practice sessions, I met a boy. I remember feeling shy towards him, but I would speak to his brother. His brother finally introduced us, and we began to talk a little during choir practice, which then turned into talks on the phone. This went on for a while. Ariel Santana was his name, and I really began to like him, and he felt the same way. My feelings were getting stronger, and I was really scared. However, I didn't feel insecure or doubtful of anything that came out of my mouth.

It was graduation day for me and my father invited him to the house for my graduation party. He reminded me so much of my father. My dad is a great husband and father, and I always wished my husband would be like "Pop," as I call him. I remember praying in the past for God to send me someone like my dad. As months went on of dating this boy from church and talking to him, my feelings were much greater.

~

A minister came up to us and cautioned us to be very careful with our marriage.

I thought I loved this guy, but then again did I really know what love was? I was allowing myself to feel different about him and not put my guard up, or so I thought. The word love was very scary for me because I wasn't sure what love really meant.

We dated for about three years and he then proposed to me. We married January 22, 1994, on a rainy Saturday afternoon. Though we loved each other, I know now that we were too young to marry.

The summer we got married I became pregnant. Two months later, I miscarried. Depression returned and the happiness that I thought I had found was now gone. Once again, I was going through the motions, doing what had to be done, because that was what was expected of me. I was applying bandages to wounds that required surgery and extensive healing (on a spiritual level). But I wasn't ready to heal yet.

My doctors said I might never be able to have children. NO

children? What type of woman would I be if I couldn't have children? Around this time, I began searching for something. I wanted to see who this God was I had heard about while growing up. My husband and I attended a special church service and from that day, our marriage became rocky. A minister came up to us and cautioned us to be very careful with our marriage. He prayed as if we were going to break up. I told my sister-in-law that he was a false prophet who didn't know what he was talking about, and I wanted to leave.

Shortly after that evening, we noticed we started to argue about insignificant things and that I was becoming distant. I would notice and comment on the petty things, and they would escalate from there. We went on with life and our arguing. I began feeling ill again, and decided it was time for a return trip to my doctor's office. To our surprise, I was pregnant. It was a difficult pregnancy, and my doctor placed me on bed rest.

In March of 1996, I gave birth to my son, Jakob Matthew Santana. He was named after two children that I had previously baby-sat and had become very close to. I ended up having a case of post-partum depression, and my hormones were going crazy. Post-partum, like my depression, was a familiar feeling. I was happy to have a baby, but I was haunted by the memory that when I was a child, I said I didn't want children. I knew my son was a blessing in every sense. He was the first grandson on my husband's side and everyone was happy. Everyone, that is, except for me. I lived my life in rewind: sick, depressed, confused, and afraid. I learned just to live that way and even began to say that I would never live to see thirty.

I had high expectations of my toddler. Everything had to be in order. I remember walking into his room and being very upset because things were not in the appropriate containers, which were color-coded. I expected perfection from a toddler. What did that say about me? I remember that day vividly. Standing there fuming about my son's lack of organization was the point I realized I had lost control. I saw the fear in my son's face, scared as I stood there yelling. Immediately, I stopped and walked out of his room.

I felt I was living in the fiery pits of hell with no way out. I was a walking contradiction. In public, I wore the mask that showed how great everything was, while behind closed doors I nitpicked about everything. I didn't understand why I was so miserable, expecting myself and everyone associated with me to be perfect. Although, if anyone from the outside came and commented on anything I was doing, I would scare them away. When it came to Jakob, I was quick to jump and became a very defensive individual that would protect my child with everything I had. Just as in my childhood and as a teen, I couldn't speak to anyone about my feelings because I felt ashamed. What would people think, say, or do if they knew the truth? I not only withheld the truth from others, I started keeping things from my husband.

Keeping my secrets, along with those of others, had a paralyzing effect on me. I found myself defending people when they were wrong and becoming a liar, which I did not want to be. While protecting the secrets of others; I became sneaky, I lied, and therefore I could not be trusted. My character was attacked because I kept the secrets of others who had sworn me to secrecy. There are some secrets that I still hold to this day, not my own, but other people's. I've held my peace in an effort to protect reputations, but I am convinced that God will one day expose the truth in His own time. I did feel vulnerable, but today it's different. I just worry about me; I do not worry about what others think of me or how they feel about me.

Marriage was hard and I felt torn by what I was feeling and what I felt others wanted of me. God was on the sidelines, right where I had left him, waiting on me. During an altar call, I saw how the people around me were caught up in the spirit of worship, seemingly at one with God. I wondered, "Lord, did you forget me? Why are you blessing everyone around me and giving me nothing? I am calling out to you crying with all that I have and nothing..." At that moment, the man that was leading the prayer stopped in front of me and said, "No, my child, I have not forgotten you."

Goodness, at that moment I began to cry like never before. How could this man know what I was thinking? I was holding my son, who was about three years old at the time. The man continued, "You and your children will help your husband in his ministry." "Your children..." Those words struck me because the doctors told me I could not have any more children, as pregnancy would mean my husband would have to pick between my life and the unborn child's life. I was full of questions. Is someone going to give me a child? Will we adopt? My goodness, how will this happen? "Your children..." I held those words in my heart, puzzled but also surprised that what I had been praying in my head at that very moment were the same ones that the man mentioned. Despite my confusion, these words ignited my faith, and I began to believe them. See what happens when you begin to listen and believe what others say and not rely on the plans God has?

I continued with life, wrong relationships, being ill, and just not really having a full committed relationship with God. I continued to live life still feeling a void, very depressed, and another attempt to take my life followed.

My marriage was becoming increasingly difficult. The more I tried to seek God, the more things would be great temporarily, and then I would spiral to a deep depression. I was serving God, learning more about having a relationship with him, but I still wasn't fully committed.

Fast forward to six years and my family was blessed by the birth of Lukas Gadiel Santana. Lukas was named after my husband's cousin and one of my favorite Christian artists. Lukas is a spunky kid with a great imagination. Yes, I have two miracles. When the doctors said, "No way," God said, "Yes." Now, what does that tell you about when others speak against you? God always makes a way. You would think I would have learned this already, but no. God allowed me to live my life, and make a mess of it, because he could see the bigger picture. He knew what He had in store for my future.

I always tell everyone God is a gentleman; he waits patiently on the sidelines till we wake up. You would think with this miracle that I would be so loving. Nope. The start of my relationship with my second son was not good in any way, shape, or form. I had a difficult delivery with Lukas, which made me not want to be near him. I knew that delivery would be painful and that I would be on medication shortly thereafter. The medication did not take and the nurses tried to keep me comfortable. What I had planned was not what happened. The pain was unbearable to the point that I was yelling at everyone. I was asking for my father, as if he could help. For some reason, I felt that if he was there all the pain would go away. He was stuck outside trying to find parking. The doctor was stuck at the light and when he did arrive he seemed to be taking his sweet time. Nothing was going well, and I felt as if I was literately going to die. When I had Jakob, I never felt this bad; this was a totally different experience.

Finally, Lukas was born in what seemed like days of struggling. Forty-five minutes passed before I would hold him, even then, I only did so because my father told me to. My older brother came up to me and told me that my son was beautiful. Everyone was excited about the new baby and wanted to hold him. Once we were home, there was very little bonding between mother and child. While holding him, I told my husband I didn't want him. His reply was, "Okay. I want him." It was hard to accept. Doctors said I had had a traumatic delivery. The baby blues had arrived, and it was a very severe case.

I began to see my doctors for regular treatment and follow ups. Mom came over for a week and would open the windows and turn music on. She had also experienced post-partum depression when she had delivered. I began to open up to one other person: Jennifer Spears, a co-worker. I explained that the doctor was treating me already. She mentioned to me how she was glad that I had told her. I went back to work almost immediately, which stunned many. I was acting as if I was really happy, always talking about my children. I was embarrassed because I had not formed a bond with my son, Lukas, but his father had. He cried with me constantly, but when my husband carried him he stopped.

The delivery was so traumatic that I held this secret anger towards him that no one knew. My body had changed drastically; I was having trouble losing weight. People thought I was so happy everywhere I went. All along, I was pretending. I was wearing this mask so no one would know what I was going through. I was a broken woman with many secrets, pains, and confusion. I would continue to confess how I wanted to die, be alone, and how I didn't understand why God would allow me to go through this.

More depression set in when others would say, "She just wants attention." Little did they know that I was dying inside, and those words that came to my ears confirmed, once again, that I did not want to not live. It took time for me to get close to my son, and it was a lot of work. It took me being alone with him for a while to renewing our relationship.

Sometimes, the only way to realize what we have is to lose it. It's incredible what you don't see yourself and that others have to tell you. I didn't want to admit to myself that something was wrong with my relationship with Lukas. I began to recognize that I was very negative towards him and chose one child over the other. God had to show me things that I didn't want to see. I am glad my love for Lukas has grown. Being a middle girl, you would think that I would be more aware of the feelings that my children were experiencing. It's very important that you know your child in all ways possible because, if you don't, then you can't relate to what they are going through.

It's odd how people change likes, dislikes, and style in general.

A year later, I began to feel my depression come on again. My relationships with friends became distant and my life with the Lord (which I thought was okay), was not where it should have been. Constantly helping others, because that was how I was raised, was always a part of me. I was looking for something, but didn't know what. I would look to others for satisfaction, in attempt to fill the voids in my life. I fell deeply into my state of depression and began attempting to take my life once more. I decided to reach out to a dear friend with what I was going through. I told him that I had taken pills. My husband came to me very upset and disappointed; my friend had told him of our conversation and what I had attempted. At this point, I became very angry because I confided in this friend, and he broke all friendship rules. He called my husband and told him that I had taken pills to take my life. In my eyes, all trust was broken.

I wallowed so deeply in my sorrows that it nearly consumed me. I smelled of death. I didn't realize what was going on with me. I felt so much rejection from those around me that I had no support from. My relationship with my husband was bad and no one wanted to be around me. I began to pray for God to give me peace. I wasn't perfect, but I knew God was the only one who could help me. Several attempts to take my life came next. Once again, I wasn't proud of what was happening to me, but I was no longer in control of my life. However, I also had never placed myself completely in God's hands.

When you trust a person and you feel that they have betrayed that trust, it hurts. In response to my hurt, I used my bitterness towards them to build a wall to keep them out. Aside from mental and emotional issues, I also continued to be sick with physical ailments. I believed this is the way that I would always be. God was permitting illness, depression, insecurities, and fear into my life. I was wallowing in self-pity on an alarming level. Good Christian women don't suffer from depression and not wanting their child. What would people think about me? People expect a perfect woman, wife, and mother. My parents would be devastated if they knew what type of mother I was. I remember my children coming home and tiptoeing through the house, whispering to one another, "Shhh! Mom is sick." I felt really bad, but I felt if I slept, it would all go away; in the morning I would feel better and these feelings would have disappeared.

As time went by, I thought that if I did something else I would feel better. I went to a local community college. By this time, my relationship with my husband was falling apart. Going through our individual problems, along with other frustrations in life, my husband and I separated twice. Before he came back the last time, we forgave each other. We were looking towards a better future together. I began my own business, which kept me busy, working late hours and away from home when he was home. Working on our relationship was difficult because we were not spending time together. This was causing a life of separation without us even realizing it.

My husband was very involved in church, and I began to get involved as well. God was teaching me so much, and I began to understand and believe that God could do something positive through me. I didn't have to be perfect, and I wasn't. I kept falling short. Unhealthy friendships and hanging out with people who were in situations similar to mine only served to add to my troubles. My relationship with my husband was crumbling. I felt he didn't understand me, which meant I would confide in those having a hard time, too. The less we communicated, the more distant I became. We lived with my depression. My husband wasn't a perfect man, but I know I was very depressed and unhappy, which didn't help our marriage at all. We lived just enough to get through the day. We never spent time together anymore. The household separated - no family vacations, no love shown.

I continued to be sick with endometriosis, which resulted in multiple surgeries. I had a final surgery, which was a full hysterectomy. Having a hysterectomy only worsened my depression, considering what I thought it meant to my womanhood. I convinced myself that I was less than a woman because I could no longer have children. My husband once said that he wanted a girl. My mind flashed back to my first child and I wondered if it would have been a girl. Add no hormones to depression, and the result is someone who feels crazy. Was I going crazy? The thoughts were overwhelming. "My husband wants a girl and I can't even give him one. God, why would you do this?" My life was rocky and I felt I had lost all of my identity.

I felt I was only a mother who was sick, confused, misunderstood, and that I couldn't find myself. I, then, decided to reach out to a lady at my church and express how I was feeling - wrong choice. She began to state that I would live the rest of my life in grief because I was a sinner. Wow, how harsh, and this was a leader that so many looked up to. I remembered the scripture that says man will fail you. I tried once more to reach out to another leader, only to be shot down again by them throwing my past in my face and listening to hearsay from family members about me.

Despite what those two women said, I began to get involved with church, and I liked it a lot. God began to work in me, but I still had so many things that were still causing confusion in my life. My marriage began to separate little by little; my past was haunting me. He was doing his thing, and I was doing my own. We both began seeking attention outside of our marriage. This went on, but then I knew what I had to do; I had to focus more on God and how he could change me. I began focusing on church, business, and family. My depression wasn't coming out anymore, I wasn't sick, and my boys were doing well. Life was pretty good, and I was very happy.

My relationship with my husband wasn't perfect, but it was good. I believed it had to be because I stopped looking at my problems and focused on other things. However, what I felt and thought was different from what my husband felt. He came to me in April of 2010 and told me he was leaving me. I was in shock, confused, and hurt. I was stunned because I thought everything was alright, and I knew I was focused and not doing anything out of line. He was determined and heartless, so that was distressing to me. He was acting as if everything that I had ever done in the past was still happening now. He left us, and I was at home with two children crying, and the three of us did not understand what was going on. I didn't have any answers for them, and I didn't know what I was going to do. I reached out to my church pastors who were very supportive and his wife played a great, big part in my spiritual walk. I didn't trust anyone except her and my mother. I didn't share everything with my parents about my situation with Ariel because I didn't want them to ever say or think negative about him. Word got to my ears that he said many things to his family about me that were not true and depression set in, once again. I didn't understand why this man that I had done nothing to didn't want to speak to me. I began to become desperate in my crying because I knew that I was innocent of what he was saying. I would share more here of what was going on with him, but it would not be my place to do so. Only he can share his testimony and experience.

Months kept going on with him living away from our home. I continued to go to my church, and God used Pastor Dee in a mighty way. She said I couldn't think about Ariel anymore and what he had or hadn't done, but that God had to do work in me. During this time, God began to work on my character. I would cry to him, and one day I decided to ask God to show me his hurt. Goodness, that was the wrong thing to ask for. God began to work in my life by stripping me out of the chains that were binding me. Little by little, he began to clean house. This was different because I understood what I needed to do and it was my choice. It was my choice to say, "Lord, take the wheel because I can't anymore; I am too young to die."

I ignored all the things that people said about me, did against me, and all past sins. I chose to fight; I chose to quit the pity party and fight for my children and myself. I continued to walk, even though family had turned against me. My character was attacked and many friendships were lost. I kept on walking, but I began to walk with my head up, not down anymore, because God was doing something in me. He cleaned all the junk that was making me smell of death. He was giving me life and I was stripped of everything; I was naked in his presence. I was holding on to and truly walking in faith. I began to pray for forty days and at the end of that time, I decided to go and fight for my marriage. One of the things my pastor said was to never have a plan B. Wow, that was an eye opener because I always had a plan B.

Going back to fight for my husband was scary, but I did it with the help of Pastor Dee. She told me she would fast and pray with me for twenty-one days. I did my part; it was one of hardest things I had ever done, but I did it. I knew God was with me. I believed that it was God who brought us together in the first place, and He alone would bring us back together. I began attending my husband's church. He refused to look at me and wanted nothing to do with me. I was still fasting, but it felt like I was being attacked by the enemy. I missed the support of my former pastors. My older son, Jakob, saw the way others treated me, and he became my protector. He didn't understand why I was fighting so hard when his father wasn't. It hurt him to see me helpless, but I had to be the example for him. God was in control, which meant sometimes I had to do things I didn't want to. Jakob had decided he was going to do the twenty-one day fast, as well. The end of the twenty-one days came, and I was done with the fighting for restoration. I was done. I told my husband, "All right, go ahead and give me the papers or whatever it is I need to sign… I'm done."

I was done with the fighting, accusations, and crying. I was giving him his freedom. God had different plans and the final word, though. God said, "No. I am giving it all back to you."

Suddenly, my husband said, "No. I am going to try 100% in this marriage." My husband didn't come back that day, though. In January, we began dating. My husband will say he doesn't like that word "dating," but that's exactly what it was. He didn't come home until August 23rd, 2011, the day we renewed our marriage vows. What a journey, right? I am so joyful and blessed that God had restored our family and marriage.

MOVING FORWARD

CHAPTER V

"But those who trust in the LORD will find new strength. They will soar high on wings like eagles. They will run and not grow weary. They will walk and not faint."

Isaiah 40:31 (NIV)

"Things have been going pretty good recently, but I honestly can't help feeling like something is going to go wrong." I know this sounds odd for someone who had seen so many great changes over the recent months, but it's exactly what I was feeling for the first few months after Ariel moved back home. I don't believe I was alone in this. I believe many in my family and some of my friends were thinking the same thing. I wanted desperately to prove all of us wrong, but I knew it wouldn't be easy.

Living as a family unit again wasn't an easy transition for us, especially for me. Part of my difficulty was in readjusting to having another authority figure under the same roof. During our separation, I had become an independent decision maker. When it came to my kids, I felt that I was the only one who should correct them. But, I wanted to see my family whole again, not just on the surface, but to its core. Change would have to begin with me, and it did. As I began to apply the lessons I learned from past mistakes, I began to notice growth in myself. As a matter of fact, our family was growing and maturing together. Learning to let bygones be bygones, I was able to release myself from experiences that had been allowed to poison my soul.

Shifting my focus from my past to making family my top priority has been very healthy for the four of us. There have been times when friends or family wanted to get together that Ariel and I decided it was best not to because our family needed to heal and become strong, something that we didn't need to have interrupted by the opinions of others. I'm not sure if they understood our reasoning or not, but this was the best decision for us at the time. We were once broken, and now that God had made us whole again, we wanted to spend time focused on one another as a couple, our children, and most importantly, God's place within our family.

As time went on, I began to understand the reasons why I had struggled so much with letting go of the things I felt had been done to me. Accepting responsibility for one's actions is a big step that many people would rather not take. When you can take this step, though, healing can begin. Just as an alcoholic must admit to themselves, first, that they have a drinking problem, every individual has free will and must use it to admit their faults. I just had to put my pride aside and accept that choices and decisions I made were incorrect and I had to let go and let God guide me. Pride was holding me back.

As is the case in everyone's life, my healing process was overlapped with the lives of others. Needless to say, some challenges were greater than others. It was from two of the most difficult instances that I learned lessons that positively impacted my life.

It was through my association with a political campaign that I was able see the scenario I could have created within my own family if I had been successful in one of my previous suicide attempts. When the campaign manager committed suicide, it opened my eyes to the struggles facing surviving family members. There was speculation as to why he did it and disagreements about who was at fault. Fighting within the family intensified, driving the division among them even deeper. At a time when they needed to show one another love and support, they were in and out of court, battling over a child. From the outside, the grieving family was a cohesive unit, but behind the scenes, they were anything but. It was difficult singing at the funeral, because I knew the truth. I knew the anger, hurt, and anguish that this family was experiencing. I began to wonder if my extended family would have reacted this way. I wanted to believe that they would never act like this, but my mom always says, "Never say 'Never.'" Believer or non-believer, it happens. Just because you have Christ in your life, doesn't mean that, when moments like this arise, you will not react with anger.

I realized that I was running from my problems and not facing things head on. God had me here for a reason, and the desperation that I felt came from my desire for a quick fix. Killing myself would only harm others, and I was being a coward. What type of footprints would I be leaving my children?

HE MUST GIVE BACK

CHAPTER VI

"I will repay you for the years the locusts have eaten..."
Joel 2:25 (NIV)

y marriage is growing in ways that I never believed were possible. The complaints and nagging have stopped. We're not perfect, but we are under construction. Now, I think before I speak, consider my husband's feelings, and have given him his rightful place as the godly head of our family. When times get bumpy, we step back and consider ways to keep things from getting any further off track. Sometimes, it's as simple as we've been doing too much and/or we need some alone time. We understand that we must work at not allowing past bad habits to derail our progress. We no longer allow negative circumstances to hinder our positive outlook or faith. We understand that God has joined us together and given us the responsibility of loving and protecting each other and our family. In Romans, the Lord speaks about evil and how it can be turned around. "And we know that in all things God works for the good of those who love him, who have been called according to his purpose," Romans 8:28 (NIV). I'm very careful not to allow negativity to enter our home. It can really kill your relationship.

There is this book called "The 5 Love Languages" by Dr. Gary Chapman. Dr. Chapman guides couples in identifying and understanding which love language they are.

1.Affirmation - which are words of praise.

2.Gifts – tangible gifts.

3.Acts of Service – "Let me do that for you" (it's in hearing this phrase).

4.Physical Touch – hand holding, kissing, pats on the back, any type of re-affirming physical contact.

5.Quality Time – spending time alone with each other.

When I look at the different love languages, I find myself high in three of them. This doesn't mean I ignore the other two, or ignore which ones my husband is. When you pay attention to the needs of your spouse, it shows you are interested in the needs and desires of the other. Marriage takes work, and, as the years go by, our likes change. However, we must be attentive to our marriage and the changes within it. This also includes our children; they also have feelings and cannot be ignored. God brought us together, and we must keep Him as a mainstay in our relationship. In a marriage, there are three people that should be involved. It will not survive with just husband and wife; God is a must, and I believe God wants us to have a healthy marriage, enjoy life, make and share great memories.

I look at my husband with lots of love and respect. Calling or sending him a message during the day, just to make him feel special. I make sure he doesn't need anything. I make every effort to let him know how I feel about him. I used to make major decisions without including him, which wasn't right. All that I desire from him, from being respected to being given his undivided attention, I give to him and it comes right back to me. By taking the time to get to know who Ariel is, I'm able to learn what he likes, what makes him tick, and to use this knowledge to become the wife he wants and deserves.

Communication is a must if a relationship is going to survive. Ariel and I have learned this lesson well, and now, we know to guard our relationship and to respect each other's feelings. *Love is what is there; love for each other.* Strengthening our family is a concept that we have extended to include our church and community. It's important to us that we diligently and compassionately serve others. As we give of ourselves to others, it has been such a blessing to see the promises of God manifesting in our lives. We are so grateful for his continued faithfulness to us.

TRUST IN THE LORD

CHAPTER VII

"Do not conform any longer to the pattern of this world, but be transformed by the renewing of your mind. Then you will be able to test and approve what God's will is—his good, pleasing and perfect will."
    Romans 12:2 (NIV)

L.E.A. of Organization is my current business and it really isn't a big priority for me, at this time, and I don't stress over it. God corrected me sternly in this area, asking me, "How can you help organize people if your life isn't even in order?" I know what God expects from me as a believer. One of my newest favorite bible verses is found in Proverbs 14:1 (NIV). "The wise woman builds her house, but with her own hands the foolish one tears hers down." My priorities have changed, and, as a result, I work my business part time. Doing this has given me the opportunity to be more involved in the lives of my children; I am able to be there for them when they want me to be there. I am so thankful to God for that opportunity.

My business is a blessing that allows me to teach my clients the need for and benefits of personal organization before attempting to organize other areas of their lives. God is a god of order, and everything we do is supposed to be done in excellence. At times, I push myself too hard, but I am learning it's okay to acknowledge when I've done my best and it's time to move forward. Because I no longer feel like I have to be in control, I can delegate work, making some aspects of work easier for myself.

Once, I attended a conference that was just what I needed. One of the speakers spoke about the different roles we play as leaders and how some of us don't want anyone else to do particular tasks. Why? Because we've convinced ourselves that if we want it done right, we must do it ourselves. Not only is this the wrong attitude to have, but it was MY attitude. I didn't realize I was burning myself out trying to do and be everything in every situation. The speaker suggested that we ask ourselves three questions: Is there someone that can do this better than I can? Can this someone produce greater results? Does this someone have time to do it? It seemed so simple: Let go and let people help you. I had managed to release four of five fingers from the grip, but I wasn't sure about fully letting go. Well, guess what? If you don't fully commit to letting go completely, it won't work.

My love of connecting with people isn't about the potential business contact. It's about finding out how I can serve them. While I make money from what I do, it's not the main reason of my business. I view mine as a platform that God has given me to help others put things in order. Currently, God is leading my business in a different direction, and I welcome it. Following God's blue print for my business is very important. Many may not pray for each decision or client, but I do. There is some shifting going on, but I welcome it, as long as he is front and center of it.

I SELECTED YOU

CHAPTER VIII

*"For you are a people holy to the LORD your God. The LORD your God
has chosen you out of all the peoples on the face of the earth to be his
people, his treasured possession."*

Deuteronomy 7:6 (NIV)

I never had many friends when I was younger, just a lot
of acquaintances, but now I am blessed with a handful
of true friends who provide godly counsel and healthy relationships, which are great for me. I have friends that I can call or send
a message to and simply say, "Pray," and, no questions asked, the
prayer chain begins. I have friends that I don't see for months or
even years at a time, but when we reconnect, it's as if we haven't
missed a beat.

Despite having had some terrible and unhealthy relationships
in the past, God has shown me how to forgive, to let go of the
hurt, and to trust again. I've come to appreciate how important it
is to always pray and ask God to show me when I need to be
careful when dealing with people, and he always does. To some
who knew me in the past, it may seem like I have become more
reserved, but I'm just being mindful. I love helping, connecting

others, and bringing *smiles* to people's faces. Why do I emphasize smiles? It's because a smile is contagious, and a smile did and still does something for me. Having hidden behind a fake smile for so long, now that my smile is genuine, I find that I can tell when someone's smile is fake.

I share my testimony because I don't want anyone to suffer like I did, or to waste time holding onto bitterness and anger to the point of thinking that suicide is their best or only option. I have had some relationships that God took away, and I thank Him for removing them from my life. Yes, I did have friends that walked away because of fear. I didn't understand, but I do now. My character was being attacked by many lies, and I stood there biting my tongue. When I was accused of agendas, not being a woman of God, and listening to how people hated me, I realized that time is important and that I didn't want to waste my breath and energy on negativity. God knows me, my heart, and my desires, and is most definitely my defender. I don't hide behind God. I walk with Him. When those who call me "friend" are gone, God is always there. I believe Jesus selected his twelve, and I select mine one by one, as well. I may not have twelve genuine friends now, but they are handpicked and selected carefully.

A BLESSING FROM GOD

CHAPTER IX

"Children are a gift from the Lord; they are a reward from him."
Psalms 127:3 (NLT)

Oh goodness, my children are my joy. The relationship I have with both is the same, yet different. With respect to love and the amount of attention I give them, everything is equal. The differences are related to their ages and their individual needs.

My older son, Jakob, was my world, especially after having miscarried my first child. We had such a close relationship and were always together. Jakob, being the oldest, saw my life as it was overshadowed by depression, arguments, and sadness. He saw, heard, and lived through what my husband and I went endured. My prayer to The Lord is that he remembers the good times, but also understands the importance of how we fought for restoration. He will know what it is like to have a broken family, yet also know what it is it to have a renewed one. Jakob will also know the supernatural miracles God performed in our family – healing my mother of leukemia, healing my father following massive heart attacks that left him with only 32% function of his heart, and the spiritual surgery he had performed on the hearts of my husband and myself. God also uses Jakob at times to remind me when I am getting too busy. Jake has grown up to be a great young man who is full of life, knowledge, compassion, and grace.

Lukas and I have such a sweet relationship. He is the child of the promise. He cannot go to bed without praying with me and giving me a big hug and kiss. God blessed me with joy and his name is "Lukas." This child is full of gladness. Rearranging my career pursuits has allowed me to be home when he gets get outs of school and be involved in all his school activities. If I miss an activity, I get the third degree and I feel horrible inside. He is a character, and so full of life and is very talented. I'm sure he will become a businessman of some sort because he can sell anything to anybody. He keeps us laughing and asks many questions that leave me dumbfounded. I know God placed these boys in my life as miracles. I, also, know they will bless many lives through their personalities and their service to God and their community.

GOD IS MY FUTURE AND HOPE

CHAPTER X

"O Lord, you alone are my home. I've trusted you, O Lord, from childhood."

Psalms 71:5 (NLT)

I don't know what my future holds, but I know God has it in his hands. I don't want to help Him, because it's unique, and if I help, I will make a mess of it. Whatever it has in store for me, I hope to never stray from it and to always keep it aligned with what He wants. I want to teach my children that you have to fight the good fight and face your trials and tribulations. I want to teach them that it's okay to walk away or hold their peace when they're being attacked. I want them to know God is our defender, but they must still face things head on. They need to understand that not dealing with their problems can be danger-ous. It is imperative that they ask God for wisdom. I want to instill in them that they can do anything they set their minds to. More importantly, I want them to know everything they have is because of God. They are both miracles that God gave me, and we are a unique family with God's DNA. They must respect themselves and others and live a godly life. They will mess up, but they must get up.

YOU ARE MY ROCK

CHAPTER XI

"For everything that was written in the past was written to teach us, so that through the endurance and the encouragement of the Scriptures we might have hope.'"
   Romans 15:4 (NIV)

What I have learned from this entire process is that God is a gentleman, what the bible says is true, and what my parents taught me as a child was what the Word said. It all comes down to making a choice: Do you want to live a life of misery or a life full of joy? I have learned that God works within me, through me, and for me. I have learned there is room for me, even when I felt there was no place in the world for me. I know there are women out there who are depressed, with no hope, feeling rejected, hurt, sick, abandoned, unloved, and persecuted. I know this because I was one. However, I also know that you can be renewed and loved, have hopes and desires, even become the woman you've always dreamt of being. But, you cannot do it on your own. You need a good support system, whether it's church, work, or a friend. Whatever you do, just don't give up. Someone cares and wants to help you. I was lost, but God was such a gentleman. God loved me so much that, when I thought all was over, he gave me life.

Pastor Dee once told me, "Until you move the elephant out of the way, you will not be able to move forward." You can't move forward with hate, bitterness, and an unforgiving spirit in your heart, because they bind you to your circumstances. You have to let them go and tell God, "No more... I need you, and I can't do it alone." I tried to fix things on my own, but at the same time, I was in the corner licking my wounds. I had to learn to forgive myself and trust that God had forgiven me. I had been hurt by so many, but instead of seeking proper treatment through God, I put a bandage on my wounds, which only hindered the healing process. When the bandage was removed, instead of healing, I discovered infection. I was now scarred and scared. One thing was for certain, if I wanted to experience a true healing, I had to be willing to let go and forgive myself. I would have to learn to love again.

NOT GOING BACK

CHAPTER XII

"Instruct the wise, and they will be even wiser. Teach the righteous, and they will learn even more." Proverbs 9:9 (NLT)

I never want to be the same person I once was. I know the past will come knocking at my door, but all I can do is hold on to God and not open the door. I became an expert at hiding my pain, but people would say I carried my heart on my sleeve, not knowing how wrong they were. Now, I deal with my situations and talk them out completely and extensively. I used to run from everything and everyone, creating a big wall that took forever to knock down. I would go to sleep upset and my husband would sleep like a baby. I am now a new person: new wife, mom, sister, daughter, friend... you name it. People may know the old me, but I introduce you to the new and improved Lea. Not the "Lea Fela," as my bullies once called me, but the Bella Lea.

I love myself, respect myself, and believe in myself. The bible says if you go back to the old, it's like eating your own vomit. Think about that for a second... Would God take everything away from me, and then give it all back, just to take it away, again? Now, that sounds crazy, don't you think? That is what people don't understand about me. They say why don't you do this, why did you walk away, you could have done this. It could have been a great platform if you waited just a little bit. No! No! No! It's not about my timing, but God's, and I will NOT compromise. I am here to warn you, God is not a joke, nor is He a toy. God will give me many opportunities to have a platform. Just as God walked among the thieves, adulterers, and murders, so do we. We don't have to point them out or say, "Get away! I can't associate with you." It's through our walk that they will see.

This is a warning to Christians to not be judgmental. God saw how I was treated and He didn't like it. We must show love, even for the sinner, because we are all sinners and fall short. We should focus on how we can help and encourage with compassion. James 3:1 (NLT) says, "My brothers and sisters, not many of you should become teachers, because we know that we teachers will be judged more strictly."

I love what it says in Matthew 18:6 (NLT). "But whose shall cause one of these little ones that believe in me to stumble, it is profitable for him that a great millstone should be hanged about his neck, and that he should be sunk in the depth of the sea." Wow, that's something to think about.

Getting to where I am now took letting go and allowing God to heal me and mold me into the woman He wanted me to be. There are those who see and acknowledge the new creation I am, but there are others, still, who view me as I was. I can't change their opinions of me. God has to do that. When I encounter people like that, it tells me that they haven't matured spiritually. My focus is where God has me now and how He is choosing to bless others through my experiences and testimony. I share my journey because I want people to know they don't have to continue living in bondage to their past. If I can help someone bypass going through years of suffering, as I did, it would be wonderful. I now understand part of the reason why I had the experiences I did. It wasn't solely for my benefit, but, also, to help others.

The woman I am today is strong, God fearing, loving, compassionate, and ready to serve. Even after reading this book, many may not understand the depth of my passion, praise, and worship of God, but it's simple; It's because of God. At my lowest point, He loved me. When I needed comforting, and was finally willing to accept it, he wrapped me in His arms, like the loving Father He is. I have a new identity as a woman full of love for God and boldness like never before.

My prayer for you is that God can make you whole. There is nothing that he can't do. If you have a marriage falling apart, are divorced, confused, depressed, suicidal, indecisive, feeling rejected, or any other number of stresses and problems, it's time you stand up and take it to God. You can take your problems to your family, friends or even doctors, but God is the ultimate doctor, healer, and restorer. No one can heal you completely like He can. He can turn that sadness into joy, your gloomy day into a sunny one. He can heal your heart, soul, and mind. When all is said and done, it's your choice, and you've got to want it. He can heal everywhere you hurt, but you must know you are not alone and make the choice to RISE. There are people going through the same trials as you. God has not forgotten you. He wants to heal you, and I want you to be encouraged, have hope, and be blessed.